Anthony Edwards

Anthony Edwards

Erin Silver

Living in THE SPOTLIGHT

CREATIVE EDUCATION
CREATIVE PAPERBACKS

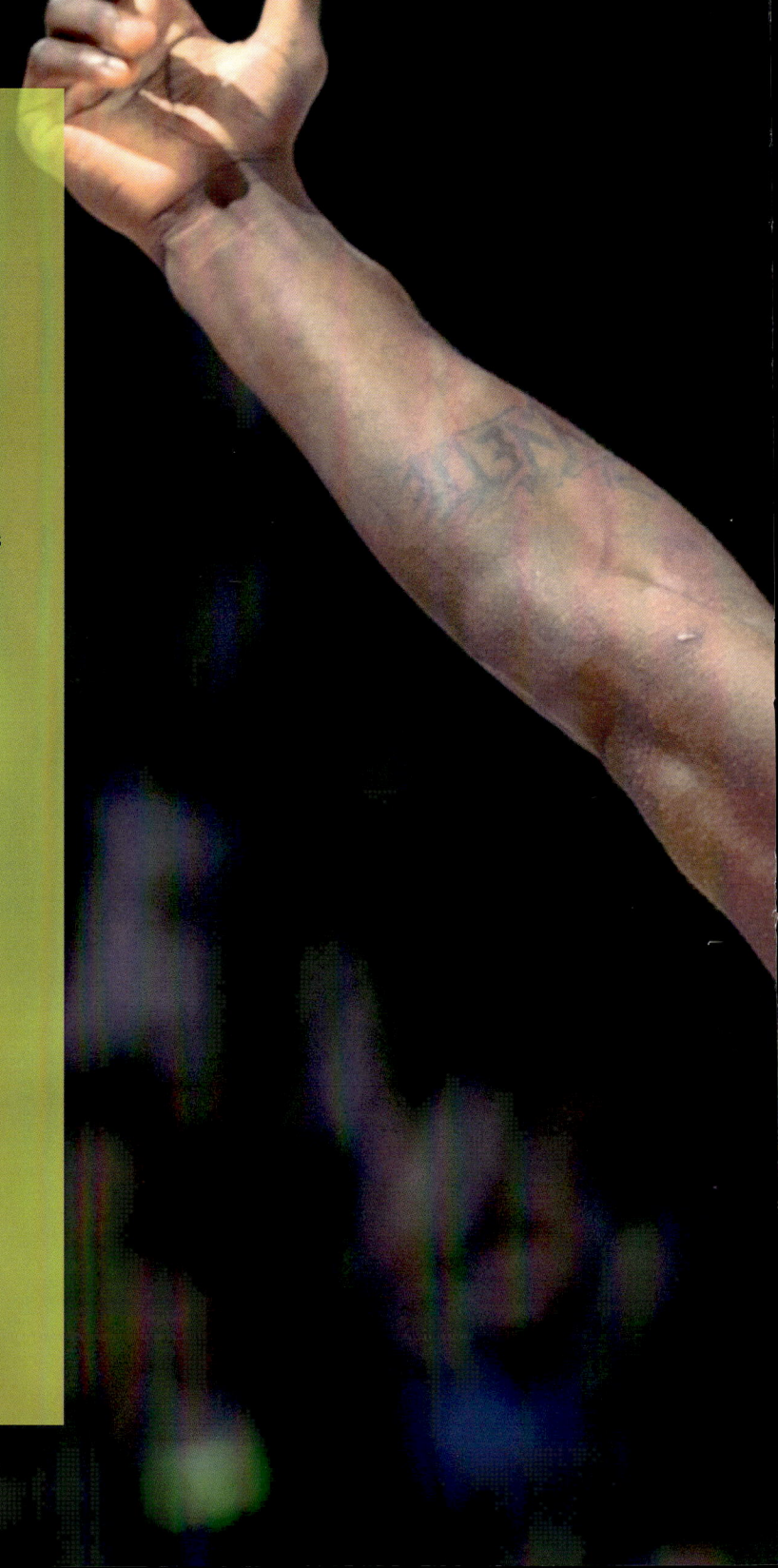

Published by Creative Education and Creative Paperbacks
P.O. Box 227, Mankato, Minnesota 56002
Creative Education and Creative Paperbacks are imprints of The Creative Company
www.thecreativecompany.us

Book design by Graham Morgan (www.bluedes.com)
Art direction by Tom Morgan

Images by Associated Press/Matt Krohn, cover; Getty Images/AAron Ontiveroz/MediaNews Group/The Denver Post, 41, Carlos Gonzalez/Star Tribune, 4–5, 6–7, 30–31, DAMIEN MEYER, 38, David E. Klutho, 17, Dylan Buell, 33, Elizabeth Flores/Star Tribune, 29, Ezra Shaw, 2, Greg Nelson, 26, John Tlumacki/The Boston Globe, 19, JORGE GUERRERO, 37, Keith Birmingham/MediaNews Group/Pasadena Star-News, 20, Kevin Liles, 13, Mark Von Holden/Variety, 43, Mert Alper Dervis/Anadolu, 23, Paras Griffin, 34, PATRICK T. FALLON, 25; Pexels/Andrii Smuryhin, 46; Shutterstock/Sean Pavone, 10; Unsplash/Danny Lines, 44; Wikimedia Commons/All-Pro Reels, cover, 45, CCS Pictures, 14, Katie Dugan/Gamecock Central, 9

Every effort has been made to contact copyright holders for material reproduced in this book. Any omissions will be rectified in subsequent printings if notice is given to the publisher.

Copyright © 2026 Creative Education, Creative Paperbacks
International copyright reserved in all countries.
No part of this book may be reproduced in any form without written permission from the publisher.
Library of Congress Cataloging-in-Publication Data

Library of Congress Cataloging-in-Publication Data
Names: Silver, Erin author
Title: Anthony Edwards / by Erin Silver.
Description: Mankato, Minnesota : Creative Education and Creative Paperbacks, [2026] | Series: Living in the spotlight | Includes bibliographical references and index. | Audience: Ages 10-14 | Audience: Grades 7-9 | Summary: "Get to know basketball star Anthony Edwards in this sports biography that showcases his athletic achievements with the Minnesota Timberwolves, personal challenges, and off-court ventures. Written for middle-grade readers, it includes table of contents, sidebars, glossary, resources, and index"– Provided by publisher.
Identifiers: LCCN 2025021159 (print) | LCCN 2025021160 (ebook) | ISBN 9798895811269 library binding | ISBN 9798896800798 paperback | ISBN 9798895812525 ebook
Subjects: LCSH: Edwards, Anthony, 2001–Juvenile literature | Guards (Basketball)–United States–Biography–Juvenile literature | Basketball players–United States–Biography–Juvenile literature | Minnesota Timberwolves (Basketball team)–Juvenile literature | LCGFT: Biographies
Classification: LCC GV884.E427 S55 2026 (print) | LCC GV884.E427 (ebook) | DDC 796.323092 [B]–dc23/eng/20250607
LC record available at https://lccn.loc.gov/2025021159
LC ebook record available at https://lccn.loc.gov/2025021160

Printed in the United States

CONTENTS

Introduction 8
Chapter 1: A Star Is Born 11
    ZOOM IN: WHY NUMBER FIVE? 14
    ZOOM IN: THE RIGHT STUFF 16
Chapter 2: Becoming Ant Man 18
    ZOOM IN: PUTTING IN THE WORK 21
    ZOOM IN: HOW TO BE A GOOD TEAMMATE ... 24
Chapter 3: Through Thick and Thin 27
    ZOOM IN: MAKING AMENDS 28
    ZOOM IN: FAN FAVORITE 35
Chapter 4: Unstoppable 36
    ZOOM IN: IT'S A GIRL! 38
    ZOOM IN: A FEW OF EDWARDS'S FAVORITE THINGS ... 40
Highlight Reels 44
    ANTHONY EDWARDS AND JUSTIN HOLLAND ... 44
    AN ALL-AROUND ATHLETE 45
    MEET ANT JR. 46
Glossary 47
Selected Bibliography 47
Websites 47
Index 48

Introduction

Wearing a red Georgia Bulldogs jersey with the number five on it, Anthony Edwards sprinted downcourt. He dribbled the ball around his opponents, then leapt over them and slammed it into the net. To cheering fans, it looked like Edwards, a 6-foot-4 (1.93-meter) shooting guard with a wingspan of 6.9 feet (2.1 m) and an average jump height of 2.99 feet (0.9 m), was born with a ball in his hands. With outstanding athleticism and exceptional ballhandling, defensive play, strength, and speed, this 18-year-old college freshman looked like a young Michael Jordan, Kobe Bryant, or Dwayne Wade. This was no wannabe baller. This was Ant Man, and he was earning himself a ticket to the National Basketball Association (NBA).

The Bulldogs were losing to Michigan State by 27 in the Southwest Maui Invitational basketball tournament. Edwards had scored just four points in the first half. It was time for him to turn up the heat. In the second half, he scored 33 more points, including seven baskets from the three-point line. It was a defining moment in his career. On that day—November 26, 2019—Edwards showed the world that he was good enough to be drafted to the NBA.

Who is Anthony Edwards, and what makes this star shine so bright?

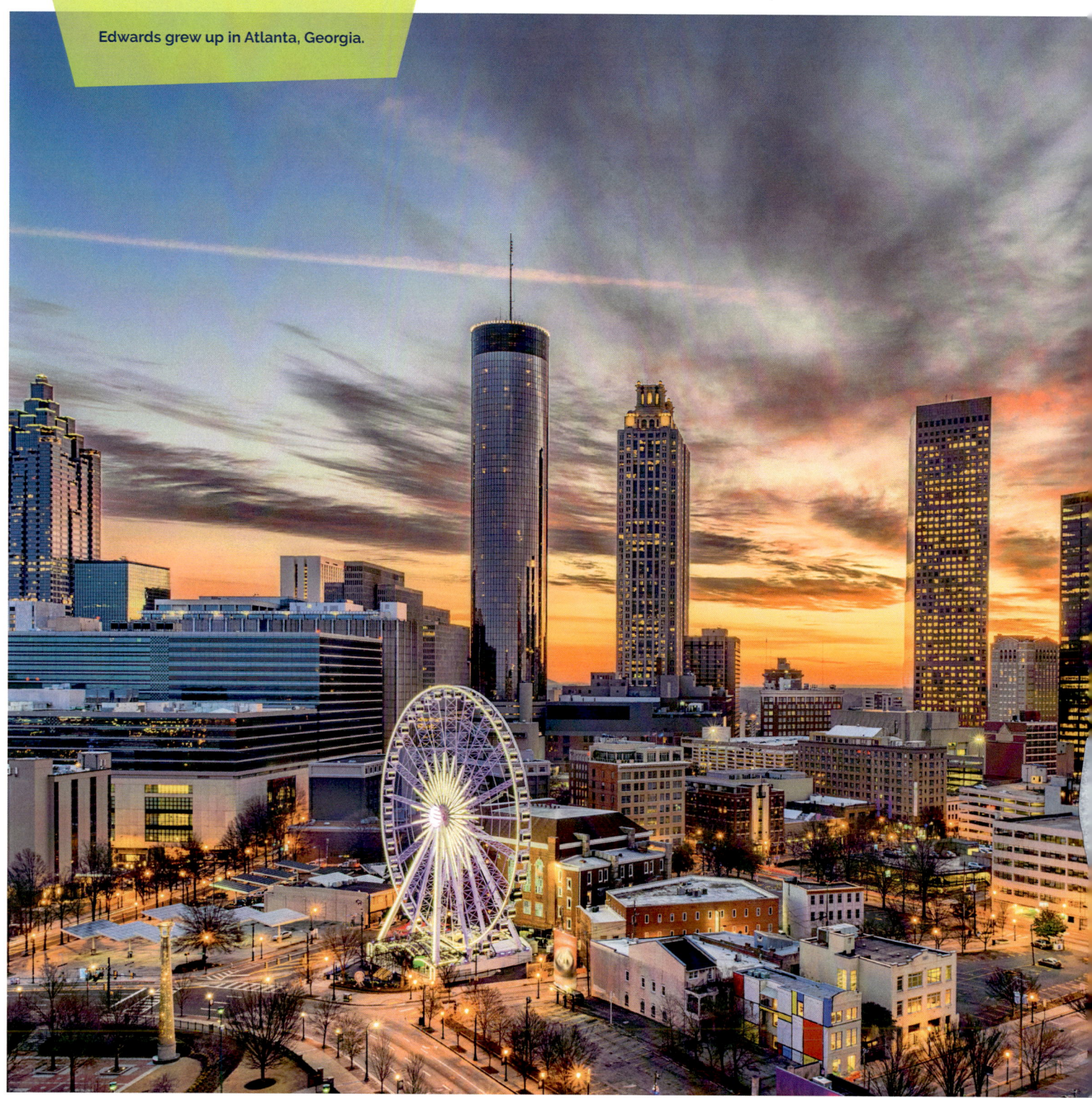

Edwards grew up in Atlanta, Georgia.

CHAPTER 1:

A Star Is Born

Anthony Edwards was born on August 5, 2001, in Atlanta, Georgia, joining three older siblings: Antoine, Antoinette, and Bubba. When he was a toddler, his father nicknamed him Ant Man. The nickname stuck, but Anthony's dad wasn't around much.

So, who raised Anthony and his siblings? His mom, Yvette, and his grandma, Shirley. Anthony's mom gave him lots of love. "And my grandma, she was like our backbone, she did everything for us," Anthony said in an interview. "When we didn't have money or lights and couldn't pay the bills, she would always come through."

Anthony and his family had dinner with Shirley every week and even lived with her for a while. Yvette and Shirley supported Anthony in all he did, especially sports. They came to all his baseball, basketball, and football games, shaking pom-poms to cheer him on. Anthony blew his mother kisses from the field. And when he sprinted for a **touchdown**, Yvette would run along the sidelines with him, giving him pointers and encouraging him to keep going.

Anthony was good at everything he played. But when he was a kid, his favorite sport was football. "I could have been a professional football player," Anthony said later. "I was really good. I was the number one **running back** in the country at nine or ten."

But every time he played basketball with his brothers in their grandmother's backyard, it seemed more fun. Anthony set himself a new challenge. "I never used to win, so I just got fed up with it. I'm like, 'One day I'm gonna beat them.'"

Anthony liked basketball so much, he decided to write himself a message—with a Sharpie on his bedroom wall at Shirley's house. He scrawled "Future **McDonald's All-American**" and "Future NBA player."

At first, Shirley was angry. But she quickly changed her mind. She told Anthony, "You're setting goals for yourself, young man. I hope you achieve it."

But soon Anthony's life would change forever. When Anthony was 14 years old, his mother died of cancer. A few months later, his grandmother died, too. They never got to see him achieve his goals.

"All our life the most supportive and loving people we had was our mom and grandmother," his brother Bubba later said in an interview. "For them both to end up passing, it was just like a strike to the heart. It turns your heart cold."

Anthony's oldest siblings became his **legal guardians**, and the family stuck together. Anthony channeled his grief and trained harder than ever. He wanted to make his mom and grandma proud. By ninth grade, he was better than both his brothers.

Edwards's hardships motivate him to be the great player he is today.

ZOOM IN: WHY NUMBER FIVE?

During high school and college, Edwards wore the number five on his basketball jersey. It represents not only his birthday, August 5, but also the dates of his mom and grandma's deaths. He wore it to honor their memory and keep them close as he played. On November 18, 2020, he sat on a couch between portraits of his mom and grandma, wearing a shirt with their names on it, while he waited to learn his fate in the NBA draft.

A young basketball trainer named Justin Holland saw Edwards's potential and took the student under his wing. Edwards could jump higher and run faster than other kids his age, but his shooting was inconsistent. Holland said, "I remember in one of the early sessions he told me, 'Coach, if I learn how to shoot, I'm going to be the best player in the country. I'm gonna be unguardable."

Holland began with the basics, training Edwards to shoot consistently. He wouldn't let Edwards shoot from the three-point line until he had proper form from a shorter distance. Edwards worked harder and became better than everyone, so he decided to **reclassify**. That way he could graduate from high school early—in 2019 instead of 2020—and play college basketball sooner.

A top **prospect** at age 17, Edwards had offers from many schools. He decided to attend the University of Georgia so he could play for basketball head coach Tom Crean, who had coached two of Edwards's favorite players, Dwayne Wade and Victor Oladipo.

Edwards also liked the atmosphere at the university, and it was only an hour away from his siblings. He explained, "I went to a game and I felt the fans in the gym, everybody showing love, and I felt like I was home," said Edwards. "My sister just had my nephew. I want to see him grow, so [staying close to home] was a big factor."

Many players were not ready to make the leap to college ball at 17, but Edwards was mature in more ways than one. He was already 6-foot-4 and a muscular 200 pounds, which meant that he could compete physically. And he felt ready emotionally as well.

"I felt like I grew up at a really young age," Edwards said. "I feel like nobody went through what I went through."

Edwards became a smooth shooter with a dunk that brought fans to their feet. He was an unselfish passer who wanted his teammates to succeed. He was popular for his charisma and his positive, likeable personality. He credited his mom and grandma with his work ethic and cheerful disposition.

"They just raised me to always keep a smile on my face no matter what," Edwards said. "I never let nobody bring me down, no matter what's going on in life. I always try to uplift people."

His performance as a Georgia Bulldog earned Edwards serious attention from the media and NBA scouts. In 2020, Edwards made up his mind: He was ready to join the NBA.

In an interview before the draft, he said, "I'm excited. I'm just ready for it to get here, for it to happen, for my family to be happy,

ZOOM IN: THE RIGHT STUFF

As a young athlete, Edwards had coaches who taught him about sportsmanship, working hard, and being humble. They also taught him the skills he needed to play well, which got him noticed. In high school, Edwards was a finalist for the Naismith Player of the Year Award. In his first game with the Georgia Bulldogs, he scored 24 points. He was later named the Southeastern Conference Freshman of the Year. TV clips of his insane dunks circulated on social media. NBA scouts couldn't help but notice this up-and-comer.

Edwards played only one season with the Bulldogs before being drafted.

and wherever I land I'm just ready to put the work in." He also told the media, "It brings joy to my heart knowing that I could get drafted and make my mom and grandma proud."

After being postponed twice because of the COVID-19 pandemic, NBA draft night finally arrived. But would Edwards be chosen in an early round? And what team would take a chance on him? Edwards would soon find out.

CHAPTER 2:

Becoming Ant Man

Edwards is quick and powerful on the court.

Edwards sat on the couch waiting for his name to be called. Even though he'd played college basketball for only one year, it was clear that he was a star. Averaging 19.1 points a game, he was the highest-scoring freshman in college and had been a finalist for several major awards. Edwards's teammates and coaches couldn't say enough nice things about him. "Edwards is one of the greatest teammates I've had the privilege of coaching," said Crean.

But his future in the NBA was not a sure thing. As one scout had said, "He's the best scorer in the draft and could be an immediate producer in the NBA with his versatility and skill set." He went on to say, "Defensively, he has the tools and physical profile to be effective, but he was undisciplined and missed assignments. Edwards showed a lack of commitment at that end of the floor."

ZOOM IN: PUTTING IN THE WORK

When Edwards began training with Justin Holland, Holland said, "If you want to be good or great, you have to be able to work through fatigue." The two spent hours in the gym on shooting, ballhandling, and other skills. "A lot of people think it comes overnight, but no, I was in the gym," Edwards said. "At midnight, you can ask [Justin Holland's] wife, she would call and be like, 'Where you at?' and he'd be like, 'I'm dropping off Ant at home, we just left the gym.' I was just working." Edwards's loss of his mom and grandmother and the need to take care of his family helped fuel him. "That just made me go harder, because I know they would want to see me at the top," he said.

The pandemic hadn't helped. Gyms and courts had been shut down. Players were unable to train or compete. The draft had been delayed five months. And other top-tier players, like James Wiseman and LaMelo Ball, were entering the draft, too.

Sitting between portraits of his mom and grandmother, Edwards waited. The Minnesota Timberwolves had been awarded the first draft pick. The struggling team hadn't played in the Western Conference finals since 2004. But when Edwards was called first overall, he was thrilled. Was this his chance to help turn the Timberwolves into a championship team?

Coach Crean thought so. "I don't think there's any question that he can be a perennial All-Star [and] in the right environment be a part of a team that's competing for championships and be an integral part of it," Crean said in an interview. ". . . But I think because of his age, because of coming a year early and all these different things, these next couple of years are going to be absolutely [important]."

Edwards didn't get to start during the first 17 games of his first season in the NBA. But he scored at least 10 points in each of his first five games. Then on January 7, 2021, Edwards scored a new career high of 26 points in one game. Finally, he'd earned his chance to become the starting shooting guard.

Edwards was a little inconsistent at first but showed signs of brilliance, including the day he dunked against the Toronto Raptors in February 2021. Footage of Edwards soaring through the air made all the sports news highlight reels after that game. Then, when two teammates were injured, Edwards stepped up. He'd grown more confident and became a leader on the team. In a March matchup with the Phoenix Suns, he scored 42 points and became the third-youngest player in the league to score 40 or more points in one game. Edwards was named Rookie of the Month several times that year. His career was looking up.

During the offseason, Edwards continued to work hard. He lifted weights and shot countless **free throws** and three-pointers. It paid off in his second season, when he scored 48 points in a November 2021 game against the Golden State Warriors. He hit a new career high of 49 points on April 7, 2022, against the San Antonio Spurs. Throughout that season, he averaged 21.3 points per game. Ant Man was only 20 years old.

Although young, Edwards shows great promise to become one of the best basketball players in history.

For all his accomplishments, Edwards became a fan favorite and was voted to the **NBA All-Star Team** in 2023. In April 2024, he hit a high of 51 points in a win against the Washington Wizards. "I don't even need to talk about how big it is. Everybody knows," Edwards said after that game. He believed he was just getting started. "I'm probably at 40 percent," he told a reporter. "I'm not even touching my prime yet." He went on to win a gold medal with the USA men's basketball team at the 2024 Summer Olympics in Paris.

Edwards has been featured on multiple magazine covers, and his clips have been viewed millions of times on social media. In addition to regular interviews with sports media, he's appeared in mainstream magazines like *Vanity Fair* and *GQ*. He can even be seen in ads, movies, streaming shows, and TV commercials, thanks to several **endorsement deals** and a shoe deal with Adidas. Edwards and his former coach-turned-business partner, Holland, started a sports content company called AE Five Enterprises. Edwards is focusing not just on basketball but on a life and legacy that includes giving back to the community.

Edwards thanks his family for his success. "I wasn't really a basketball guy growing up, but watching [Bubba], I decided to follow

ZOOM IN: HOW TO BE A GOOD TEAMMATE

Edwards is known as an unselfish player—he doesn't always have to be the star of the show. "I love to pass the ball," he said. "I get electric when I make a pass or somebody else makes a pass and when a teammate scores." He encourages others and is the first to congratulate a teammate. Former Bulldogs teammate Tyree Crump said, "If your day is going bad, he can put a smile on your face. He cares more about somebody else than he cares about himself." These traits have earned Edwards respect and admiration from everyone who meets him.

Edwards speaks to a crowd of reporters in a post-game press conference.

in his footsteps," Edwards said in 2023. "If it wasn't for him, I wouldn't be up here. I just want to thank him."

Edwards has kept his family close to him throughout his journey. "I just don't trust people," He explained. "The people I came in with is the people I'm gonna stay with. I'm not adding no other people to my circle. I think that's the point of having siblings, is to be there for each other."

As for Bubba, a rapper who goes by the name bdifferent: He's thrilled to see his baby brother in the starting lineup of every game. "It's like a dream," Bubba said. "I'm watching a live dream."

BECOMING ANT MAN — 25

CHAPTER 3:

Through Thick and Thin

Edwards was making headlines before he was even drafted to the NBA, and they weren't always positive. In November 2020, he told the press, "To be honest, I can't watch basketball. I'm still not really into it. I love basketball, yeah. It's what I do." Then he said he'd pick football over basketball if he were drafted to the NFL. "Because you can do anything on the field," he said. "You can spike the ball. You can dance. You can do all type of disrespectful stuff." In the NBA, Edwards said, "you can't do any of that. You'll get **fined**." He also said he'd like to be a rapper like his brother Bubba.

Edwards and his friends and family later explained the comments. Edwards meant he'd rather play basketball than watch it. He also meant that football is special to him because that's where his sports

Edwards fights his way through a tough defense to score for his team.

> **ZOOM IN: MAKING AMENDS**
>
> Ant Man is learning from his mistakes. After offending the LGBTQ+ community, he made a donation to Queerspace Collective, which helps LGBTQ+ people who are dealing with harassment, homelessness, and isolation, which can lead to suicide. "Just try to right my wrongs," Edwards told the media. "You know, give back, show them that it's no hate. You know what I'm saying? It's all love." As Timberwolves coach Chris Finch later shared about Edwards's ongoing personal growth, "It's clear that the education and maturity of Anthony Edwards continues to be a work in progress."

journey began, and it was the sport his mother and grandmother watched him play before they died.

But after Edwards joined the NBA, he said other things that were harder to explain. In September 2022, Edwards shared a homophobic story on Instagram. His 1.2 million followers heard him laughing at a group of gay men and using antigay slurs. Edwards apologized. "What I said was immature, hurtful, and disrespectful, and I'm incredibly sorry," he wrote. "It's unacceptable for me or anyone to use that language in such a hurtful way, there's no excuse for it, at all. I was raised better than that!"

Edwards took the story off his social media and made a donation to an LGBTQ+ youth organization, and the NBA fined him $40,000. The president of the Timberwolves released a statement saying the organization was "disappointed" in Edwards's behavior and that "the Timberwolves are committed to being an inclusive and welcoming organization for all and apologize for the offense this has caused to so many."

Edwards still has a lot to learn as a young NBA player.

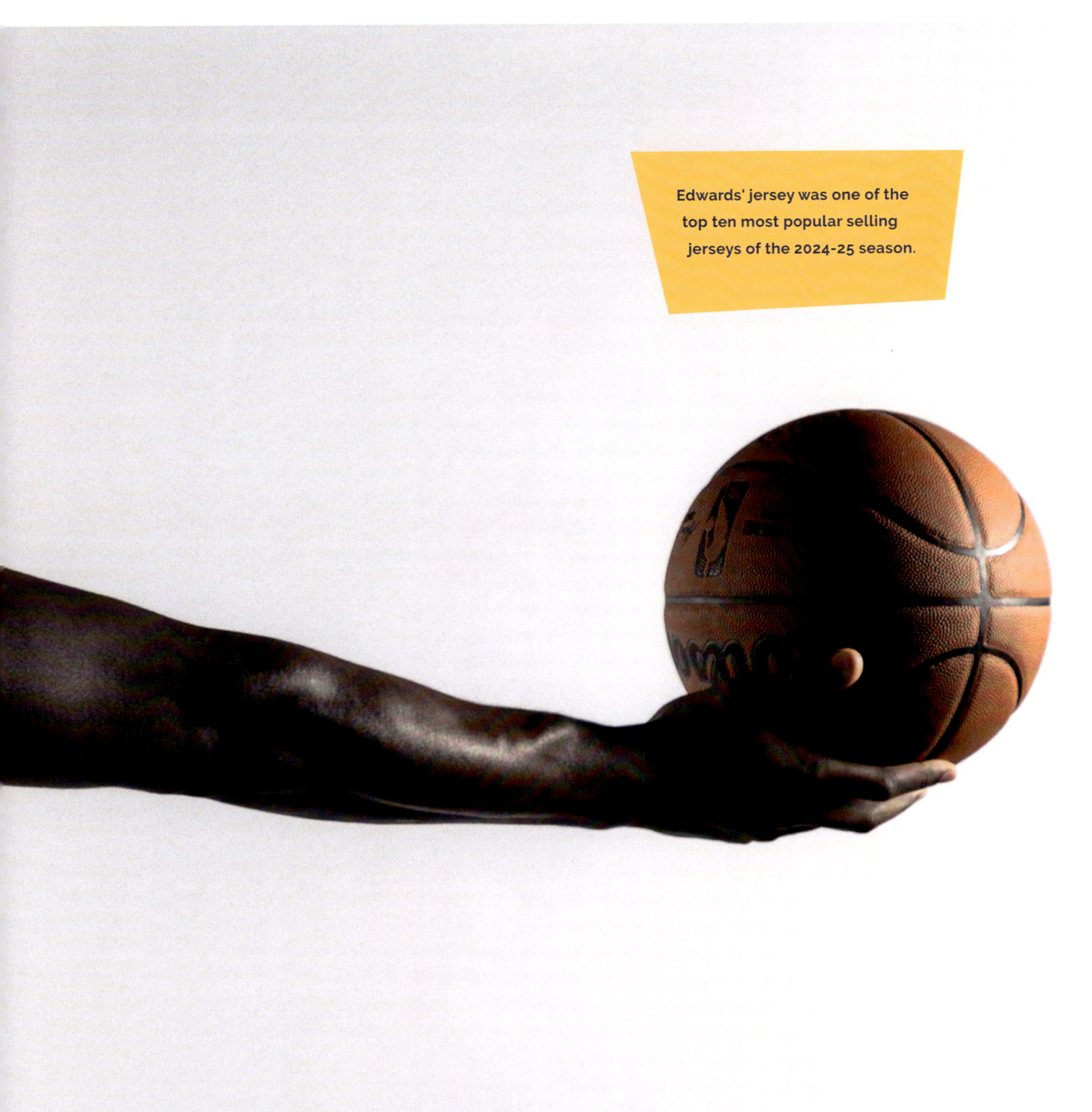

Edwards' jersey was one of the top ten most popular selling jerseys of the 2024-25 season.

In January 2024, Edwards was fined another $40,000 for publicly criticizing NBA officials after a tough game against the Oklahoma City Thunder. The Timberwolves pulled off a win, but Edwards didn't think all the calls were fair. He complained that the referees had cheated. "I'm gonna take the fine, because the refs did not give us no calls tonight," he said. "We had to play through every bump, every grab. I don't know. I don't know how we won tonight. Big shoutout to my team, big shoutout to my coaches, for sure."

In fall 2024, Edwards received backlash for a *Wall Street Journal* interview that was insulting to some NBA legends. "I didn't watch it back in the day, so I can't speak on it," Edwards said of the earlier era of basketball. "They say it was tougher back then than it is now, but I don't think anybody had skill back then. [Michael Jordan] was the only one that really had skill, you know what I mean?"

Nine-time NBA All-Star Paul George wasn't happy. During a podcast, he said, "I thought it was kinda disrespectful for the game . . . I thought it was a very immature comment. Obviously, Anthony Edwards is super talented, and he's a huge talent going forward. But just how much the game has grown, you gotta pay dues to those dudes that did it before us."

Another former pro player, Rasheed Wallace, added, "Ant-Man is a skilled player. I love his tenacity. I love the dog in him. But here's the thing, you also got to be respectful with it. Just do your homework. Do your history," he said.

Edwards skillfully dunks over his opponent.

Perhaps the biggest of all his controversies happened in December 2023. A woman who claimed she was pregnant with Edwards's baby shared private texts from Edwards online. In the texts, he pressured her to get an **abortion** and offered her money in exchange. To address the headlines, Edwards said, "I made comments in the heat of a moment that are not me, and that are not aligned with what I believe and who I want to be as a man," he said. "All women should be supported and empowered to make their own decisions about their bodies and what is best for them. I am handling my personal matters privately and will not be commenting on them any further at this time."

Edwards and his grandfather Ben Edwards.

> **ZOOM IN: FAN FAVORITE**
>
> Despite his negative news stories, Edwards is still a fan favorite. People love his gravity-defying dunks and social media posts in which he raps, dances, and jokes around with his family or teammates. Fans say he's funny, that they like his personality and even his Adidas shoes. But maybe most importantly, his actions speak louder than words. He always shows up ready to play, even through injuries, and he gives every game his best effort. As Timberwolves head coach Chris Finch said, "Ant is a fierce competitor . . . He's a gamer. He loves to play."

Through all the ups and downs, Edwards and his siblings have supported one another. Their difficult experiences have only brought them closer together. Older brother Antoine said of Edwards, "He took [the deaths of his mother and grandmother] and started excelling in basketball afterward. It took a toll on him, but . . . it made him stronger. It made him push harder. It turned his game to a whole different level."

While Edwards pursued his basketball dreams, he helped his brother Bubba chase his own dreams. Before performing during game six of the Timberwolves versus Nuggets playoffs in May 2024, Bubba said, "I appreciate the opportunity, and it's just a blessing, man. I can't really call it too much, but a blessing. I get to do what I love in front of thousands [of] people."

Bubba said Edwards pushes him to keep recording his rap songs. "He's on my head all the time about sending new songs, you know, because he like to get hyped before the game," said Bubba. "So, he pressures me on sending new songs and stuff like that. So, he's super supportive."

CHAPTER 4:

Unstoppable

Edwards is one of the star basketball players featured in season two of the NBA App original series *Pass the Rock*. He's seen laughing with his grandfather and joking around with his siblings as he talks about his rise from backyard basketball to the NBA.

"My family was all sports," Edwards said. He shared how he and Bubba used to get up at 6:00 a.m. to play basketball. At age 15, he started working hard and improved a lot. When he won his first game against his brother, it was a big deal. "I ran around the whole school celebrating and telling everyone," Edwards laughed.

Though the grief his family experienced is still hard, "it makes it easier that we got each other," Edwards said. "My older siblings

Edwards hangs from the hoop after making yet another of his famous dunks.

ZOOM IN: IT'S A GIRL!

Family means a lot to Edwards. On March 1, 2024, Edwards left the Timberwolves' game against the Sacramento Kings at halftime to be with his girlfriend, Shannon Jackson, during the delivery of their daughter, Aislynn. "That's my baby girl!" he said proudly after she was born. "It's my happy day." The two accompanied Edwards to the Paris Olympics, where they smiled for a photo wearing Team USA clothing. Fans look forward to seeing more photos of Aislynn as she continues to grow.

Anthony Edwards and LeBron James on the podium after winning Gold at the Paris 2024 Olympic Games.

took care of me and make sure I was all right. The point of having siblings is to be there for each other."

Edwards still remembers what it was like growing up with little money and so much loss. That's why he started a nonprofit organization called Don't Follow the Wave (DFTW). Its mission is to educate student athletes on potential career paths while they pursue their athletic dreams. In addition to education, DFTW provides mentorship, exposure, and networking opportunities. Edwards also likes helping single moms, since his mom worked so hard to care for her children on her own. He enjoys the youth basketball programs he created in partnership with Adidas, called Edwards Edwards Five (AE5). The program provides teams and camps for players in elementary through high school. He tells players, "What you put in, you get out."

Edwards also leads by example. As successful as he's been in basketball so far, he believes it's important to have a career outside of the sport. He and his former trainer, Holland, started Three-Fifths Media in 2019. The company produces documentary, sports, and competition shows. In 2023, Edwards signed on with a sports management agency called WME Sports. His WME team negotiates Ant Man's endorsement deals and helps with his businesses and charitable work. "I've been locked in to giving everything I have to be the best I can be on and off the court, and no one is better equipped to support me and my family through this journey than WME Sports," Edwards said. "I'm excited about all we will do in basketball, entertainment, business, and philanthropy, and as I look at the legacies of other WME athletes, I know there is no limit to what's possible."

His business ventures continue to grow. In 2024, Three-Fifths Media signed a deal with an entertainment company called Wheelhouse to produce sports-related content that will appear on streaming services and TV. "I love the business we're building

Edwards fights to earn points for the Timberwolves, shooting over Nikola Jokic of the Denver Nuggets.

ZOOM IN: A FEW OF EDWARDS'S FAVORITE THINGS

In a video for *GQ* magazine, Edwards explained that he loves the color blue, Yeezy slides (because he likes to be comfortable), Chester Hot Fries chips, his deck of cards (to play his favorite game, spades), and a speaker so he can listen to his brother, Bubba, who is his favorite rapper. He loves his diamond AE5 logo chain; he wears it to games and with his friends, but only one chain at a time. He also loves his 13-pound bowling ball. He keeps a favorite photo of his mom on his phone. "She was my number one fan for sure." Finally, he loves his English bulldog, Ant Jr. "He's the best in the world," said Edwards. "I love him."

and the content we're-creating, and this partnership with Wheelhouse will help us take a big step forward," Edwards said.

It seems Edwards is everywhere: on the court, behind the scenes, and on screens. In 2022, he was featured in *Hustle*, a basketball movie starring Adam Sandler. In 2024, he appeared as one of the NBA stars in *Starting 5*, a documentary-style Netflix sports series that takes a look at life behind the scenes in the NBA. Edwards is the new face of Sprite's "Obey Your Thirst" campaign. He also has endorsement deals with Fanatics and Bose. When Edwards signed a $50 million contract extension with Adidas, he also became the face of that brand—and has the hottest basketball shoes on the market with his Adidas' AE 1s. In 2023, he signed a five-year extension with the Timberwolves worth more than $200 million—plus another $45 million available in incentives. Those numbers could go even higher by the 2028–29 season. It is likely that Edwards and his family will never have to worry about money again.

> **Edwards's basketball story is just beginning. His team continues to improve, and his statistics are only getting better.**

Edwards and his family can't believe how far they've come. "It's always been a dream, but it's never been a fact that we knew he was going to make it," Bubba once said. Now, he says he gets chills to think of what they've accomplished.

When asked what his mom and grandmother would think of his success, Edwards was quick to answer. "They loved to see me win," he told the *New York Times*. "When I was little playing football growing up, I always won the championship in football or basketball. They want to see me win. When I win and get a ring or a gold medal for Team USA, I think they'll be super excited."

Though he's already reached one of these goals, he's not nearly done yet. With only a few NBA seasons under his belt, Edwards's basketball story is just beginning. His team continues to improve, and his statistics are only getting better. When he retires from basketball one day, Edwards says, he wants to be remembered as "the best guy to be around, one of my favorite teammates and a winner. That's it."

Edwards at the premier of *Hustle* in 2022.

UNSTOPPABLE — 43

Highlight Reels

ANTHONY EDWARDS AND JUSTIN HOLLAND

Sometimes an athlete gets to work with a coach who changes their life dramatically. For Anthony Edwards, that coach was Justin Holland, a basketball skills trainer who had played college basketball. Edwards was in eighth grade when they were introduced by a family friend. Their first workout together was hard. Edwards wanted to quit. But he kept going back. He liked being challenged and became addicted to working hard. The two spent hours training together throughout Edwards's high school years. Holland even worked with Edwards to prepare him for the NBA draft.

Today, the two are as close as ever. Holland is Edwards's business partner and manager. They work together on things like parent company AE Five Enterprises and Three-Fifths Media, which creates sports documentaries and short films, like Showtime's *Get Yours* and *Ain't Doing Enough*.

"We don't want to just be an athlete," Holland said in an interview. "We want to show the next generation how to come in the game and build a business around your brand. If we can do that, everything will be trending in the right direction for our youth."

The two have many more deals in the works. They also make time for their community initiative Don't Follow The Wave. Holland said, "People think he's ascending so fast, but it feels a lot different internally, because we know how much work we've been putting in behind the scenes for everything moving forward."

Expect more good things to come from their friendship.

AN ALL-AROUND ATHLETE

Edwards excelled at football and baseball from a young age. As he got older, he discovered he was great at pretty much every sport he tried. After long training sessions with Holland, they decided to mix it up and play table tennis, just for fun. Edwards was no good at first and lost every

game. But within a week, he'd practiced so much that he could hit forehands and backhands and put spin on the ball. He even studied table tennis shots on YouTube, the way he studies the moves of other basketball players.

Then he developed a love for bowling. Though he started playing only a few years ago, his scores are high enough to be a professional bowler. (A consistent score of 200 or more is professional level.) "If I got my ball, I'm throwing a 180, for sure," Edwards said in an interview. "Every time I go, I'ma crack 200 at least once."

In another interview, he said he was also good at tennis, swimming, lacrosse, and golf. "Whatever you need me to do I'm gonna go do it!" he joked, even adding hockey, trash-can ball, and cooking to the list of things he'd be "A1 from Day One" at!

In a separate interview that went viral, Edwards said he might one day play in the NFL. "If I win a ring in the next three-four years, I'm going to play football." That hasn't happened yet, but Edwards is so confident in his skills that it very well could.

MEET ANT JR.

Edwards loves his English bulldog, Ant Jr.—named after himself. He jokes that the dog can do everything he can do. The dog goes everywhere with Edwards—to the gym, to the stadium, to bed, and even to the bathroom. He wears AE jerseys and was photographed wearing Edwards's favorite AE gold chain. They celebrate National Pet Day and Christmas together. Edwards even had an artist paint a portrait of Ant Jr.

Fans love to follow Ant Jr. on Instagram, X, and TikTok. In fact, the dog has more than 200,000 followers on Instagram alone. His social media features photos and videos of Pops, as Edwards likes to call himself, and Ant. Jr. hanging out at photo shoots, at basketball games, with fans, beside the Timberwolves mascot, and at home. In one video, Ant Jr. predicts the men's and women's NCAA brackets.

Edwards got Ant. Jr. in 2021. He describes Ant. Jr. as loyal: "He's the best dog in the world. He's my best friend. He's the best thing that happened to me as far as joining the NBA. If I ever have a bad game, I go home and he's always there."

Research shows that having a pet can reduce stress and anxiety, ease loneliness, and even improve physical and mental health. It's no wonder an athlete with a high-pressure job loves to go home and cuddle with his pet!

Glossary

abortion—ending a pregnancy

backlash—a strong negative reaction

charisma—magnetic charm or appeal

contract extension—a legal agreement to continue a contract

dunk—when a player leaps through the air and slams the basketball into the net

endorsement deals—when a brand or company pays a famous person to represent them and be featured in ads, on television, and so forth

fined—made to pay a financial penalty

free throws—shots at the basket awarded because of opponents' fouls; worth one point each

homophobic—against people who are gay

legal guardians—people who are legally responsible for taking care of a child

LGBTQ+—an umbrella term that includes sexualities like lesbian, gay, bisexual, transgender, and queer or questioning

McDonald's All-American—an honor for exceptional high school basketball players who are chosen to compete in a special tournament

NBA All-Star Team—a special game featuring the league's 24 top players as chosen by fans, media, and players

NBA draft—an event when basketball prospects have the chance to be chosen to play on an NBA team

prospect—an athlete scouts look at to potentially draft to a professional team

reclassify—to graduate in a different year than your age group typically graduates

running back—a football player who carries the ball up the field and is part of the offensive team

scouts—people who recruit athletes for professional teams

tenacity—refusal to give up

three-point line—an arc on a basketball court from behind which a shot is worth three points

touchdown—one way a team can score in football, usually worth six points

Selected Bibliography

Collier, Jamal, "Anthony Edwards, Justin Jefferson and Minnesota's Iconic j=Jersey Swap," *ESPN*, October 22, 2024. https://www.espn.com/nba/story/_/id/41909688/anthony-edwards-justin-jefferson-garnett-moss-photo.

Daniels, Evan, "Self-Made Man: How Anthony Edwards Became an Elite NBA Prospect," *247Sports*, January 3, 2020. https://247sports.com/college/basketball/recruiting/Article/Self-made-man-How-Anthony-Edwards-became-an-elite-NBA-prospect-141553138.

Geoffreys, Clayton, *Anthony Edwards: The Inspiring Story of One of Basketball's Star Guards*, Calvintir Books, 2024.

Krawczynski, Jon, "Anthony Edwards' Rise: The Big Brother, Big Lights and Big Dreams That Inspired Him," *New York Times*, July 11, 2023. https://www.nytimes.com/athletic/4681279/2023/07/11/anthony-edwards-brother-contract-timberwolves-star.

Scarborough, Alex, "The Pain and Promise of Top NBA Draft Prospect Anthony Edwards," *ESPN*, November 15, 2020. https://www.espn.com/nba/story/_/id/30321844/the-pain-promise-top-nba-draft-prospect-anthony-edwards.

Sports Illustrated. "The Power List: The 50 Most Influential Figures in Sports," *Sports Illustrated*, December 2024. https://www.si.com/sports-illustrated/power-list-2024.

Index

Adidas, 24, 35, 39, 42
AE Five Enterprises, 24, 44
All-Star Team, 24
Ant Man Jr., 40, 46
Anthony Edwards Five, 39
awards, 16
backlash, 28, 32, 34
brother (Antoine), 11, 35
brother (Bubba), 11, 12, 24, 25, 27, 35, 36, 40, 43
Crean, Tom, 15, 21, 28
Don't Follow the Wave, 39, 44
draft, 8, 14, 16, 17, 18, 21, 27, 44
daughter, 38
endorsements, 24, 40, 42
Finch, Chris, 28, 35
football, 11, 12, 27, 43, 45
Georgia Bulldogs, 8, 16, 24
grandmother, 11, 21, 28, 35, 43
Holland, Justin, 15, 21, 39, 44, 45
Hustle, 42, 43
Jackson, Shannon, 38
legal guardians, 12
LGBTQ+, 28
Minnesota Timberwolves, 21, 28, 32, 35, 38, 42, 46
mother, 11, 12, 21, 28, 35, 43
Pass the Rock, 36
personal life, 11, 12, 38, 40, 46

philanthropy, 40
scouts, 16
sister (Antoinette), 4, 11
Starting 5, 42
Three-Fifths Media, 38, 44
Wheelhouse, 40, 42
WME Sports, 40